Don't You Dare Touch Me There

by
S. L. Walker

This book is dedicated to my beautiful, brave, and unapologetically untouchable girls Brionna and Sienna. You are
the center notes in every song my heart sings.

I have certain ways I don't like to be touched.
And, sometimes people like to touch me too much.
When that happens I politely say,
"I don't like to be touched that way."

Like when mommy tells me to hug her friends,

I just want to hold my breath until it ends.

I wonder if I'll get in trouble if I say

"I don't like to be touched that way."

My family members let my cousins sit on their knees. I say, "No thanks, that's not for me."

Sometimes they frown, but that's okay. I just don't like to be touched that way.

Strangers ask if they can touch my hair.
And, I dont want their hands up there.
"It's not that serious!" they sometimes say.
I still don't like to be touched that way.

There are body parts I cover with my bathing suit at the pool.
If someone tried to touch me there, that would not be cool.

My friends and I call those parts by different names.
But when it comes to being touched there, we all feel the same.
Our bodies belong to us and it's our right to say "Dont you dare touch me that way!".

Your body is yours. It belongs to you.

So, don't let anyone touch it if you don't want them to.

Fellow Parents and Caregivers:

Thank you for investing in this wonderful conversation starter about touch. My ultimate goal with 'Don't You Dare Touch Me There' was to make sure children are comfortable saying "hands off". I also wanted to encourage parents to allow children to make the important decision of determining their own touch boundaries.

My hope is that as you journeyed through the pages of the book with SiSi, it sparked meaningful and open dialogue about unwanted and inappropriate touch. These early conversations will promote body safety and hopefully reduce the risks of childhood trauma.

Thank you again for your purchase. I hope you enjoyed reading this book with your child as much as I enjoyed writing it.

S.L. Walker

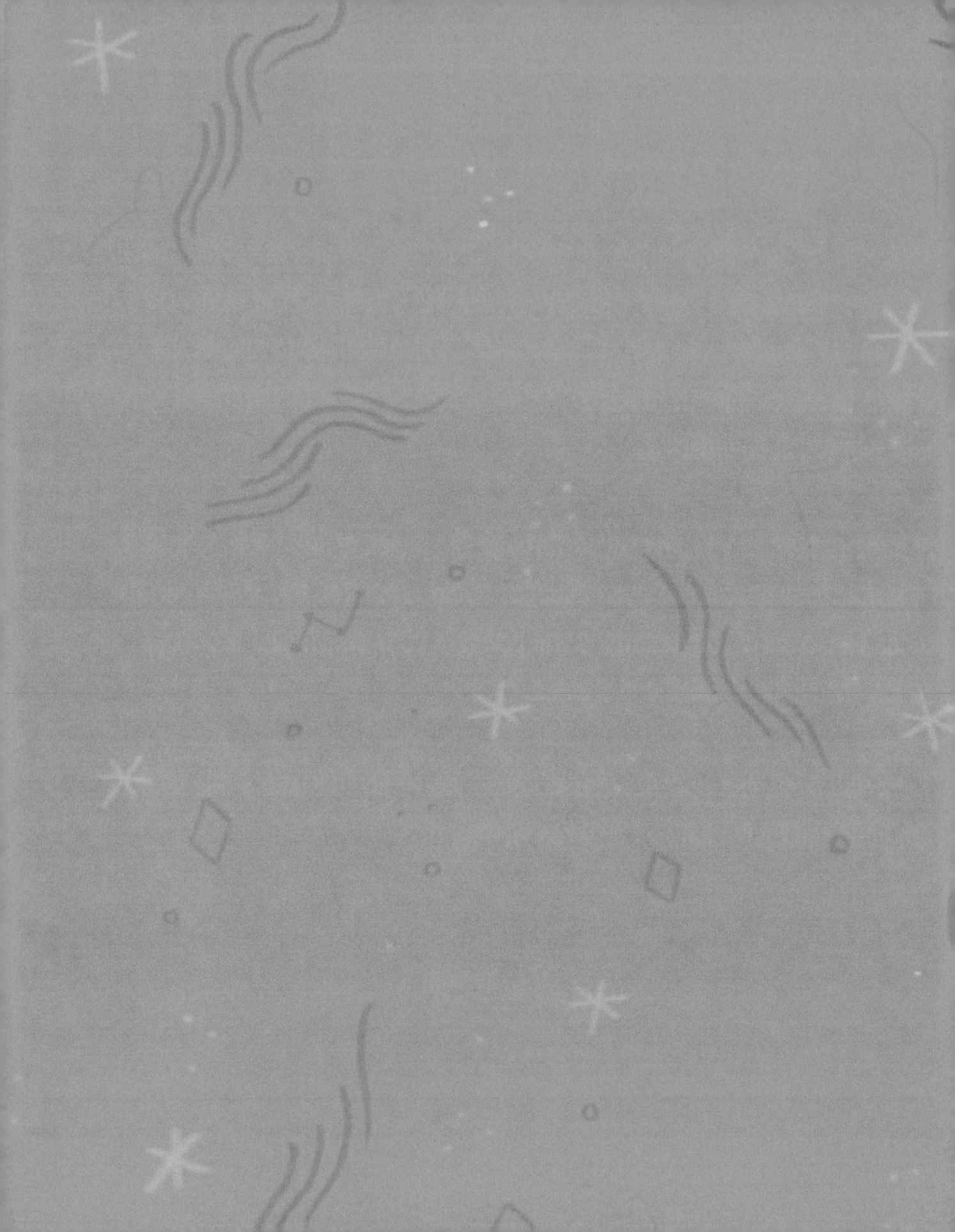

Copyright © 2019 by Suzettra L. Walker

This is a work of creative nonfiction. Some parts have been fictionalized in varying degrees, for various purposes.

All rights reserved. No part of this publication may be reproduced, distributed, or transmitted in any form or by any means, including photocopying, recording, or other electronic or mechanical methods, without the prior written permission of the publisher, except in the case of brief quotations embodied in critical reviews and certain other noncommercial uses permitted by copyright law.

Made in the USA
Columbia, SC
11 May 2019